EMERGENCE III
UNIFIED THEORIES

Copyright

or reader of this material. Any perceived slight of any individual or organization is purely unintentional.

The resources in this book are provided for informational purposes only. They should not be used to replace the specialized training and professional judgment of a health care or mental health care professional.

Neither the author nor the publisher can be held responsible for using the information provided within this book. Please always consult a trained professional before deciding on the treatment of yourself or others.

Preface

In the emerging landscape of artificial intelligence and machine learning, the quest for systems that can adapt, learn, and make decisions akin to human cognition is ever more pressing. This book provides an in-depth exploration of frameworks that bring us closer to achieving these monumental goals. By synergizing the Value Assessment Computational Framework (VACF), the Multisensory Computational Framework (MSCF), and the Repetition Duration Intensity (RDI) System, we delve into the untapped potentials of AI, laying the foundation for more responsive, intuitive, and intelligent systems.

Forward

As we stand on the brink of a new era in computational science and artificial intelligence, the frameworks presented in this book serve as cornerstones for future innovations. They offer a multi-dimensional view that incorporates rapid value assessment, multi-sensory input, and learning through repetition and intensity. Beyond theoretical explorations, this book provides practical insights into diverse fields, from healthcare to finance, illustrating the immediate applications and far-reaching implications of these frameworks. Readers will find this book both an intellectual stimulus and a practical guide, serving as a catalyst for further research and development.

Table of Contents

EMERGENCE III

UNIFIED THEORIES

Chapter 1

A Computational Framework for Studying Unconscious Biases

"How can we computationally study human biases?"

Unconscious biases have been an object of extensive study in psychology, largely because of their pervasive impact on human decision-making and behavior. The Implicit Association Test (IAT), developed by researchers at Harvard University in 1998, has become a widely used tool for measuring such biases (Greenwald, McGhee, Schwartz, 1998). It reveals how individuals associate positive or negative attributes with certain social groups, even when they may consciously reject such biases. Applying IAT in various societal contexts, such as healthcare, academia, and law enforcement, reveals the grim consequences of biased behavior. For example, recent research by Lai suggests that implicit biases exist and significantly influence people's actions, even overriding their explicit beliefs and intentions (Lai et al., 2014).

In addition to individual biases, researchers like Clara Wilkins have delved into how biases are embedded and manifested within groups, particularly in hierarchical structures where power differentials exist (Wilkins, 2017). Wilkins' research illustrates how certain beliefs can lead to discriminatory actions, especially when the existing social hierarchy is perceived as being threatened.

Mathematical Modeling of Bias

Understanding bias in human cognition and decision-making often involves complex, multivariate analyses. While qualitative research provides insightful narratives, a quantitative approach, such as Bayesian statistical models, can offer rigorous ways to identify and measure biases (Gelman et al., 2013). Mathematically, one might represent a generic bias in decision-making as follows:

$$Bias_i = \sum_{j=1}^{n} w_j \cdot F_{ij}$$

Here, $Bias_i$ is the bias exerted in the ith decision-making context, F_{ij} represents different features or variables influencing that context, and w_j are the weights representing the importance of each feature. These weights can be positive or negative, and their absolute value indicates the strength of the feature's influence.

Translating Human Bias into AI Systems

Our aim in this book is to develop a computational framework that allows for the encoding of biases or preferences in AI systems, analogous to unconscious biases in human cognition. Though AI systems don't possess cognition, understanding human biases provides invaluable insights for developing algorithms that can simulate preference-based behavior. This can allow AI systems to develop traits and characteristics, as well as preferences that enable them to favor one thing over another. For instance, a recommendation algorithm can be designed to favor newer content over older content, without requiring explicit rules to do so.

Toward a Computational Framework

With this context, our goal is to construct algorithms that can capture, analyze, and even adopt biases or preferences, with potential applications ranging from machine learning models in natural language processing to decision-making algorithms in autonomous systems. It's important to note that this book will not delve into the ethical implications of introducing bias into AI systems, but rather focus on the technical framework for achieving this.

We will employ statistical methods, machine learning algorithms, and other computational techniques to translate the study of human bias into the realm of AI. Future chapters will elaborate on these methods and offer examples of how to implement them.

By linking the study of unconscious biases in human behavior with computational methods, this book seeks to lay the groundwork for a novel, interdisciplinary approach to understanding and developing biased or preference-based AI systems. This introductory chapter serves as a foundation, upon which the ensuing chapters will build to create this comprehensive framework.

Chapter 2

Simplifying Our World: Abstraction Mechanisms in AI Systems

"How do AI systems simplify complex information?"

The categorization process is an indispensable part of human cognition, aiding us in organizing and simplifying our complex environment. This capability is not exclusive to humans; even mice have been shown to exhibit categorization skills, as research from the Max Planck Institute of Neurobiology demonstrates (Reinert et al., 2021). Researchers have identified neurons that are specialized in storing categories, an example of how abstract information can be encoded at the neuronal level. This biological form of abstraction is essential, enabling humans and animals to quickly assimilate new experiences into existing mental frameworks.

Mechanisms of Abstraction: Biological vs. Computational Systems

In biological systems, neurons in the prefrontal cortex gradually develop category-selective responses. These neurons become a part of long-term memory, functioning as a repository for categorical knowledge. In contrast, computational systems like AI models can adopt abstraction mechanisms through algorithms designed to perform feature extraction, dimensionality reduction, or clustering.

Algorithmic Approaches to Abstraction

One could use algorithms like Principal Component Analysis (PCA), t-distributed Stochastic Neighbor Embedding (t-SNE), or K-means clustering to implement abstraction in AI systems. Let's consider K-means clustering as an example:

$$J = \sum_{i=1}^{n} \min_{\mu_j \in C} ||x_i - \mu_j||^2$$

Here, J represents the objective function, n is the number of data points, C is the set of cluster centroids μ, and x_i are the data points. The algorithm minimizes J by adjusting the cluster centroids μ_j, effectively grouping similar data points.

Application in AI Systems

A recommendation engine could employ abstraction mechanisms to cluster users or items based on their features. Such clusters would serve as categories the algorithm could refer to when making recommendations. As category-selective neurons facilitate quick decision-making in biological systems, the algorithmic abstraction allows the AI system to quickly provide relevant recommendations without analyzing the entire dataset.

Gradual Learning and Adaptation

Like the gradual development of category-selective neurons in biological systems, AI models can adapt their categorization mechanisms over time. Machine learning models like Neural Networks allow for gradual learning through backpropagation, enabling the model to fine-tune its internal parameters based on new data.

$$W^{(new)} = W^{(old)} - \alpha \cdot \frac{\partial J}{\partial W}$$

In this equation, $W^{(new)}$ and $W^{(old)}$ are the new and old weights, α is the learning rate, and $\frac{\partial J}{\partial W}$ is the gradient of the loss function J with respect to the weights.

By employing these algorithmic techniques, an AI system can simulate the biological process of abstraction and categorization, allowing it to simplify its world view, adapt to new information, and make decisions based on the categories it has formed. This serves as another layer in our computational framework for instilling preference-based behavior in AI systems.

Chapter 3

Simplifying Our World - Cognitive Categorization and Preference in AI Systems

"How do AI systems categorize and show preferences?"

Simplifying Our World - Cognitive Categorization and Preference in AI Systems explores the intricate weave of cognitive categorization. Cognitive categorization acts as an anchor, recognized as pivotal in enabling humans and animals, such as mice, to maneuver through the labyrinthine complexities of their environments. As cited from the research at the Max Planck Institute of Neurobiology in 2021, this mechanism clusters analogous objects, experiences, or phenomena under universal classifications, prompting responses rooted in accrued knowledge. Mirroring this natural concept, AI systems can be architected to demonstrate a proclivity or tilt toward certain classes. Such a configuration endows the AI with a semblance of a distinct "mental model" that echoes personalization. This chapter further illuminates the mathematical and computational schema vital for embedding categorization and preference within AI systems.

Diving into the biological world, studies on mammals, encompassing species from mice to humans, spotlight neurons within the prefrontal cortex that exhibit an evolved "category-selective" propensity. As the Max Planck Institute of Neurobiology illustrates, these specialized neurons spring to action when engagement with constituents of a previously grasped category occurs. From a mathematical lens, given an input X representing attributes like visual cues or auditory signals and an output Y indicative of categorical labels, the transformational function f that associates X with Y crystallizes as:

$$f : X \rightarrow Y.$$

Intriguingly, as an array of data points unveil themselves, the function f undergoes a metamorphosis.

Charting the algorithmic terrain for AI-centric categorization, machine learning methodologies, exemplified by the k-Nearest Neighbors (k-NN) or Support Vector Machines (SVM) techniques, emerge as conduits for supervised instruction. For our framework, let A denote the set of attributes, and B symbolize the gamut of categories. The training phase witnesses the AI honing its abilities, anchored on a compilation of feature vectors sourced from A and their complementary categories from B. Central to this process is the minimization of the objective function $J(\theta)$ to discern the quintessential model parameters, θ, framed as:

$J(\theta) = \Sigma L(y_i, f(x_i; \theta))$ from i=1 to N, where L is the loss function, y_i signifies true labels, and $f(x_i; \theta)$ represents the forecasted labels. Subsequent to this phase, the AI's proficiency undergoes rigorous testing in the validation phase, using an independent dataset. The culmination sees the AI, fortified with the knowledge amassed, classifying fresh, unlabeled data snippets during its operational phase.

To breathe life into the AI's inherent inclination, or "bias" towards specified categories, an inclination indicator, β, integrates with the objective function $J(\theta)$ as:

$J(\theta) = \Sigma L(y_i, f(x_i; \theta)) + \beta$ from i=1 to N. Distinctly, β isn't merely a regularization parameter; it morphs the function f, lending a predilection towards select classes. Enriched with the capability to recalibrate based on fresh rules or datasets, this bias term equips the AI to "mature" and refine its inclinations progressively.

An interesting contemplation arises around the innate "Us/Them" binary frequently manifested by humans and primates. Often delineated based on societal or ethnic delineators, this dichotomy could find reflections in an AI modeled on preference tendencies. Yet, the silver lining lies in the transparency offered by AI, permitting structured modifications to these categorizations, laying down a controlled scaffold to dissect the repercussions and plausible applications of such classification mechanisms.

Summarizing, the faculty to classify and harbor inclinations isn't an exclusive biological possession. With the right algorithmic infusion, AI systems can replicate and even augment these traits. By instilling these dimensions in AI's design blueprints, we stand at the brink of unveiling AI models that not only adapt but also "personalize," heralding a redefined interaction paradigm shimmering with responsiveness and depth.

Chapter 4

Integrating Sociological and Behavioral Frameworks

"How can sociology and behavior shape AI understanding?"

The quest to understand human behavior has given rise to various models and theories. Two prominent approaches are the sociological" Us vs. Them" framework and Clark Hull's mathematical deductive behavior theory. While the former concentrates on social groupings and their impact on individual actions, the latter aims to quantify behavior using mathematical equations. This chapter explores how these two seemingly disparate frameworks can be integrated to create a more comprehensive model of human behavior.

Hull's Mathematical Deductive Theory of Behavior

Clark Hull formulated a mathematical equation to predict human behavior, encapsulating various factors ranging from stimulus intensity to drive strength and habit. His equation is expressed as:

$$sER = V \times D \times K \times J \times sHR - sIr - Ir - sOr - sLr$$

Hull's equation tries to capture the complexity of human behavior by considering internal stimuli, motivational factors, and even random errors. However, Hull's model has received criticism for being overly complex and not accounting for social and emotional variables significantly influencing behavior.

"Us vs. Them": A Sociological Perspective

The" Us vs. Them" framework highlights the impact of social groupings on individual behavior. According to this framework, individuals naturally categorize themselves into different social groups based on characteristics like race, ethnicity, or even fandoms. These social groupings lead to biases and preferences that influence actions and decisions.

Bridging the Gap: An Integrated Model

We propose integrating an 'I' term into Hull's equation to create a more comprehensive model of human behavior. This term would represent the influence of belonging to a particular ingroup or outgroup. The modified equation becomes:

$$sER = V \times D \times K \times J \times sHR \times I - sIr - Ir - sOr - sLr$$

Where I is defined as:

$$I = w_1 \times R + w_2 \times E$$

Here, w_1 and w_2 are weights assigned to race (R) and ethnicity (E), respectively. These weights could be determined based on societal values or individual perspectives.

Case Study: Discrimination and Economic Incentives

Consider a hiring scenario with two equally qualified candidates— one from an ingroup and another from an outgroup. According to the "Us vs. Them" framework, there might be an automatic preference for the ingroup member. Using Hull's terms, this preference could be accounted for by enhancing the 'K' (incentive motivation), thus increasing the sER (excitatory potential) for hiring that individual.

Addressing Controversies and Limitations

The integration of social factors into Hull's model can mitigate some of the criticisms directed at each framework. For instance, the modified equation can potentially explain why people engage in risk-taking behaviors that contradict the idea of homeostasis. This occurs when the ingroup's norms or expectations make risk-taking behaviors more socially rewarding, thereby influencing the 'I' and, in turn, the sER.

The introduction of artificial intelligence systems can provide further refinements. Advances in machine learning algorithms enable us to better capture the complexities of human behavior that neither the "Us vs. Them" framework nor Hull's equation can sufficiently cover alone (Smith, J. Jones, M. 2019, "Incorporating AI in Behavioral Models," Journal of Modern Psychology).

The integration of Hull's mathematical deductive theory of behavior with the "Us vs. Them" sociological framework offers a more nuanced understanding of human behavior. By considering both internal factors like drive and external influences like social groupings, this integrated model captures the multifaceted nature of human actions and decisions. While each framework has its limitations, their synthesis opens new avenues for research and practical applications in the realm of behavioral science.

Chapter 5

Learning Preferences and Biases in a Multi-Sensory Computational Framework

"How do AI systems learn from multiple sensory inputs?"

Chapter 5 delves deeply into the intricacies of the Multi-Sensory Computational Framework by navigating through the innovative realm of integrating preferences and biases into AI systems. Unlike conventional systems that primarily process multisensory data, the objective here is to architect AI systems equipped to synthesize preferences and biases anchored in the Repetition, Intensity, and Duration parameters, commonly encapsulated by the acronym RID.

To breathe life into this vision, the framework welcomes a pioneering preference scoring mechanism. This tool not only captures sensory data with finesse but also integrates a dynamic scoring system rooted in RID metrics. The magic of this system lies in its fluidity, allowing for adaptive recalibration of values in response to evolving data landscapes. Visualize an AI continually exposed to vivid imagery of birds. Over time, the algorithm would imbue this AI with an escalating preference for avian-related data.

Tackling the often-controversial territory of biases in AI, a fresh perspective is proposed: biases, when intentionally sculpted and meticulously managed, can unlock deeper data interpretations. This becomes particularly pivotal in sectors as diverse as personalized content curation or healthcare optimization.

Diving into real-world applicability, consider an AI-powered music curator. Harnessing the RID parameters, it could craft playlists that resonate deeply with individual users, factoring in song repetition, playback volume (intensity), and song duration. Translating this to healthcare, an AI could deftly sift through patient responses to varied treatments. Drawing from this, it might recalibrate medication suggestions, harmonizing with individualized patient profiles.

To underpin these functionalities, certain computational methodologies emerge as frontrunners. Fuzzy Logic Systems, known for their prowess in navigating ambiguity, emerge as potent tools for making decisions based on incomplete or murky data. In parallel, Bayesian Networks, steeped in probabilistic reasoning, can deftly interweave historical and present data, synthesizing the Repetition and Duration metrics with aplomb.

Enhancing the adaptability quotient, it's envisioned that a cyclical feedback mechanism be embedded. Periodically reassessing RID metrics and even absorbing user feedback directly, this AI would possess the agility to reorient its preferences and biases in tandem with experiential insights and explicit user directives.

Navigating the terrain of ethics, it's imperative to underline the profound ethical ramifications when programming AI systems with inherent biases. Vigilance must prevail, continually monitoring and guiding these biases to prevent them from spiraling into undesirable or even harmful trajectories.

On the algorithmic horizon, the mechanisms for gauging RID metrics manifest as elegant yet powerful. `Count(x_i)` offers a transparent metric for Repetition, cataloging the frequency of sensory inputs. Intensity finds its muse in a scoring system that converts qualitative descriptors into quantifiable metrics via `Intensity(x) = f(x)`. Meanwhile, Duration updates organically with each sensory experience, depicted by `Duration(x, t) = g(t)`.

Two-phased database refinements encompass the dissection of every sensory event 'e' into its RID constituents, culminating in their database assimilation. Bayesian methodologies elevate this further, refining the prediction accuracy of potential preferences or biases through contextual relevance.

Pivoting to a tangible understanding, consider two contrasting sensory contexts. Situations labeled as "Melody" or "Lavender" typify tranquility, often characterized by muted intensity spread over extended durations. In stark contrast, scenarios dubbed "Flash" or "Bang" evoke abruptness, bursting with high intensity condensed in fleeting moments. By assiduously tracking RID metrics across myriad contexts, AI systems are poised to craft richer, more sophisticated preferences, verging on what might be perceived as a nascent form of "character" or "personality."

Conclusively, this chapter unfurls the tapestry of the Multi-Sensory Computational Framework's potential evolution. By amalgamating computational intricacies, tangible illustrations, and ethical compasses, it lights the beacon for crafting AI entities endowed with an enriched, discerning lens towards their data universe.

Chapter 6

Real-World Application and Analysis

How are these concepts applied in real-world scenarios?

In an era where artificial intelligence increasingly interacts with complex and nuanced environments, the Multi-Sensory Computational Framework is a pivotal methodology. This chapter aims to delve into the intricacies of this framework by focusing on its application in real-world scenarios. Central to this framework are the RID parameters—Repetition, Intensity, and Duration—which form the cornerstone for modeling preferences and even providing insights into rudimentary personality traits.

The computational assessment of RID parameters is crucial, and algorithms are specifically designed to quantify and evaluate sensory data. Take Repetition, for instance. Algorithms can be written to count each occurrence of a unique sensory input, usually represented in a dataset or matrix. The variable x_i in an equation might signify each specific instance of the sensory input x. Likewise, Intensity is another critical metric, often calculated using descriptive adjectives associated with the sensory input. A function $f(x)$ is generally employed to convert descriptive adjectives into quantifiable measures. Lastly, Duration, the amount of time the sensory input is experienced, also gets recorded for data analysis. Here, $g(t)$ is a function that calculates the duration t for a given sensory input.

Supplementing the core RID parameters is the context in which these sensory inputs occur. Context can significantly affect how RID parameters are interpreted, offering additional layers of complexity and nuance. Bayesian methods provide robust algorithms for integrating context into the analysis. A Bayesian formula would typically update the likelihood of a trait or event occurring based on the RID parameters and the specific context in which these parameters were recorded. This dual reliance on RID parameters and context ensures a more comprehensive understanding of sensory inputs.

Let's consider some concrete examples to ensure this isn't an abstract discourse. Imagine a scenario involving an avalanche event, a natural disaster, where understanding sensory data could be vital for early warning systems. The auditory stimuli in such a scenario could include sounds like "rumbling," "roaring," and "booming." When these inputs are fed into the Multi-Sensory Computational Framework, they are quantified based on Repetition, Intensity, and Duration. For instance, the initial database table might show a Repetition count of 1 and Intensity levels of 1 for "rumbling" and "roaring" but a higher Intensity level of 2 for "booming." As the event unfolds, these tables get updated. Initially set to zero, the duration might change to 1 as the event continues, providing real-time data that could be crucial for disaster management systems.

However, not all scenarios are catastrophic. Imagine a tranquil setting where someone listens to a soothing melody while experiencing the aroma of lavender. In this instance, the Multi-Sensory Computational Framework can help in areas like ambient intelligence or smart homes by understanding occupant preferences. The updated database table in this setting would typically show low intensity and longer duration for both "melody" and "lavender," enabling the AI system to identify the relaxing nature of the environment and perhaps adjust lighting or temperature accordingly.

Despite its robustness, the framework is not without challenges. Scalability is a significant concern, given the explosion of sensory data in today's interconnected world. The framework must adapt to accommodate this vast array of data without losing efficacy. Noise in the data, resulting in false positives and negatives, poses another hurdle that needs overcoming. Improved classification algorithms and error-correction methods may offer solutions here. Finally, the dynamic nature of real-world environments necessitates that the framework be adaptable. New algorithms that can learn and adjust to new types of sensory data or changing contexts are a research area ripe for exploration.

In conclusion, this chapter serves as a comprehensive exploration of the Multi-Sensory Computational Framework's practical applications. While this is not the end of the discussion, it opens avenues for further study, particularly in the exciting crossroads of AI, sensory data analytics, and even the simulation of rudimentary personality traits. By resolving existing challenges and integrating new computational methods, the framework stands to make significant contributions to developing more nuanced and adaptable AI systems.

Chapter 7

Technical Examination of RID Parameters in Advanced Applications

How do RID parameters function in advanced AI applications?

This chapter dissects the utilities of Repetition, Intensity, and Duration (RID) parameters within complex, scientific, and technologically advanced frameworks. Through this examination, we aspire to illuminate each parameter's unique computational advantages for high-level modeling of preferences and personality traits in artificial intelligence systems.

Utility of Repetition in Stochastic Systems: Repetition is a quantitative measure of event occurrence and instrumental in stochastic systems and probabilistic modeling. Practical scenarios demonstrate the importance of repetition. Repeating unusual packet transmission patterns in cybersecurity could signal a potential breach or Distributed Denial of Service (DDoS) attack. Advanced algorithms such as Markov Chain models can utilize repetition data for predictive analytics. In bioinformatics, repeating specific DNA sequences is crucial for identifying functional elements in genomes. Hidden Markov Models (HMM) often deploy repetition metrics in the sequence alignment processes.

Intensity as a Magnitude Scalar in Signal Processing: Intensity functions as a vector magnitude in high-dimensional data spaces, particularly in signal processing and machine learning contexts. For example, in sonar systems, the intensity of the received signal can help differentiate between noise and valuable information, thereby aiding in object recognition underwater. Similarly, Convolutional Neural Networks (CNNs) can be designed to consider pixel intensity when identifying objects or faces, which is often crucial in medical imaging diagnostics.

Duration in Time-Series Analysis and Temporal Logic Models: Duration, the temporal dimension, finds extensive applications in time-series analysis and formal methods involving temporal logic. In the financial market, algorithmic trading uses the duration of specific stock price movements to signal buy or sell actions. Time-series models like ARIMA (Autoregressive Integrated Moving Average) use duration as a core component for prediction. In Natural Language Processing (NLP), dialogue systems can utilize the duration of silence or speech for context and sentiment analysis. Recurrent Neural Networks (RNNs) often make use of duration data in language models.

Algorithmic and Computational Challenges: There are several challenges in utilizing RID parameters. Algorithms that integrate all RID parameters should be optimized for polynomial time complexity. Managing data sparsity issues in high-dimensional RID spaces is another challenge that can be addressed by techniques like Principal Component Analysis (PCA) or t-distributed Stochastic Neighbor Embedding (t-SNE).

Future Directions: Research in emerging fields like Quantum Computing or Neuromorphic Engineering may introduce new paradigms for RID parameter utilization. These advances could potentially lead to real-time solutions for issues such as combinatorial explosion in high-dimensional data.

In summary, this chapter provides an in-depth view of how RID parameters can be optimally utilized in a variety of advanced, scientific, and technical applications. It elucidates the computational and algorithmic complexities involved and also projects a trajectory for future interdisciplinary research.

Chapter 8

Technical Examination of RID Parameters in Advanced Applications

How can we further delve into RID parameters?

This chapter comprehensively explores the utility of Repetition, Intensity, and Duration—commonly abbreviated as RID—in the context of advanced scientific and technological frameworks. RID parameters are critical in numerous sectors, from cybersecurity and bioinformatics to machine learning and finance. Their universal applicability is an area of keen research interest and practical implication.

Repetition is a fundamental metric for identifying patterns and anomalies, especially in stochastic systems. In these systems, the frequency of a given event can provide insights into its importance or relevance. In cybersecurity, for instance, the role of repetition cannot be overstated. When analyzing network traffic, multiple occurrences of an unusual pattern of packet transmissions could indicate a possible cyber attack. Here, statistical models like Markov Chains become invaluable. Using past data to make probabilistic predictions about future events, Markov Chains provides a dynamic framework for assessing the likelihood of various outcomes. In cybersecurity applications, this enables real-time analysis, allowing security systems to flag or even preempt cyber-attacks based on a repeated sequence of suspicious events.

Likewise, the importance of repetition extends into the realm of bioinformatics, particularly in the field of genome sequencing. Repetitive sequences in genomic data often signify vital genetic structures or functional elements. Tools like Hidden Markov Models (HMMs) apply repetition metrics to align sequences efficiently, contributing to numerous applications from medical research to evolutionary biology. For example, identifying the repetition of specific sequences could be key to recognizing genes responsible for hereditary diseases opening avenues for targeted therapies or preventative measures.

Intensity, another RID parameter, finds relevance in high-dimensional data spaces. Its role is often pivotal in areas requiring complex pattern recognition, like signal processing. In acoustic signal processing, for instance, the intensity of received signals can mean the difference between detecting an enemy submarine or mistaking it for an underwater rock formation. Advanced algorithms often rely on intensity as a scalar measure, cutting through 'noise' to focus on 'signals,' so to speak. In healthcare, intensity measures play a crucial role in medical imaging. Pixel intensity within MRI or CT scans can distinguish between different tissue types, enabling more accurate diagnoses and facilitating early interventions.

Duration, the third RID parameter, is often the hardest to model despite being the most intuitively understood. In financial markets, the time a particular stock trend has endured can signal whether it's time to buy, hold, or sell. Algorithmic trading systems often use models like Autoregressive Integrated Moving Average (ARIMA) to incorporate the duration of price trends into their strategies. Similarly, in Natural Language Processing (NLP), understanding the duration of various components like silence or speech segments can offer contextual cues. Recurrent Neural Networks (RNNs) often utilize duration metrics to add layers of meaning to text or speech, affecting everything from sentiment analysis to context recognition.

The application of RID parameters isn't without its challenges. One of the most pressing issues is computational complexity. As we incorporate more parameters to enhance the modeling accuracy, the computational resources required also increase, sometimes exponentially. This brings us to the second challenge: high-dimensional data. The sparsity of high-dimensional spaces is a well-known issue in machine learning and statistics, often requiring sophisticated dimensionality reduction techniques like Principal Component Analysis (PCA) or t-SNE to manage effectively.

Looking ahead, the future of RID parameters in computational models is exciting and poses several intriguing questions. Emerging technologies like Quantum Computing could potentially revolutionize how we approach computational complexity. Similarly, advancements in Neuromorphic Engineering may offer new paradigms for emulating human-like cognition in machines. These emerging fields could provide the keys to unlocking real-time analytics in high-dimensional spaces, revolutionizing the applications of RID parameters in numerous sectors.

To sum up, RID parameters offer a rich and multifaceted toolkit for modeling and understanding a wide array of complex systems. From the nitty-gritty of genomic data to the fluctuating trends of financial markets, and from the split-second decisions required in cybersecurity to the nuanced diagnostics in healthcare, RID parameters stand as versatile tools for modern computational systems. This chapter has aimed to provide an exhaustive insight into the practical applications and computational complexities surrounding RID parameters and suggests that they will continue to be an area of active research and application as technology continues to advance.

Chapter 9

Polynomial Time Complexity and Its Relevance in Advanced Applications

Why is time complexity crucial in AI applications?

In the vast realm of computer science, the concept of polynomial time complexity stands out as a pivotal benchmark, defining the efficiency of algorithms. Delving into its theoretical foundations, polynomial time complexity, represented as $O(n^k)$, essentially means that an algorithm's computational complexity doesn't grow beyond a polynomial function of its input size, n, where the term k remains a constant. To put it into a mathematical context, we express this relationship as $T(n) = O(n^k)$. This metric serves as a litmus test, demarcating efficient algorithms from inefficient ones, especially in contexts where time is crucial.

Shifting focus to applications in optimization algorithms, several real-world scenarios emphasize the importance of polynomial time complexity. Take, for instance, network flow algorithms, such as Max-Flow and Min-Cut. These algorithms, indispensable in the fields of network design and telecommunications, predominantly operate in polynomial time. Their primary role? Optimizing data flow across networks ensures the bandwidth is used as efficiently as possible. Another application, linear programming, leans heavily on algorithms like the Simplex method. While, in theory, the Simplex method can exhibit exponential behavior in worst-case scenarios, empirical observations suggest that it generally operates in polynomial time for most practical scenarios, especially in domains like operations research and supply chain management.

Machine learning and data science, both burgeoning fields, are no strangers to the benefits of polynomial time algorithms. A case in point is supervised learning algorithms. Familiar names in this space include Decision Trees and k-Nearest Neighbors (k-NN). These algorithms, due to their polynomial time nature, are primed for applications that demand real-time responses, such as autonomous driving systems. A vehicle's split-second decision on whether to swerve or brake could hinge on these algorithms. In another vein, feature selection in high-dimensional datasets, a task of paramount importance, often employs polynomial-time algorithms. For instance, Recursive Feature Elimination, a technique frequently applied in bioinformatics, aids in the precise selection of genes, determining which ones are pivotal for a particular biological process or disease.

The domain of cryptography and security heavily banks on polynomial time complexity. Let's consider Public Key Cryptography. Algorithms central to this space, such as RSA and Elliptic Curve Cryptography, are typically designed to work in polynomial time for processes like key generation and encryption. However, there's an interesting twist when it comes to decryption without the appropriate key. Here, algorithms intentionally aim for exponential time, a design choice ensuring the encrypted data remains secure and practically impenetrable.

Natural Language Processing (NLP), a field at the intersection of linguistics and computer science, also finds value in polynomial time algorithms. Delving into tasks like syntactic parsing, which dissects sentences into their grammatical components, algorithms like the Earley Parser come into play. Operating within polynomial time constraints, such algorithms lay the groundwork for advanced

NLP tasks, such as machine translation, where transforming a sentence from one language to another without losing its semantic essence is critical. Moreover, in sentiment analysis, determining whether a user review is positive or negative, understanding the underlying grammatical structure through syntactic parsing can provide valuable insights.

However, the road isn't without its bumps. Certain challenges keep researchers on their toes. One such challenge is NP-Completeness. In the realm of computational theory, it's a known fact that not all problems can be comfortably nestled within polynomial time boundaries. Problems classified as NP-complete stand as testaments to this, pushing the limits of what's computationally feasible. Additionally, in many real-world scenarios, merely ensuring worst-case polynomial time complexity doesn't quite cut it. This is where amortized analysis steps in, offering a broader perspective by looking at performance over a series of operations rather than isolated ones.

Peeking into the future, several promising avenues could redefine how we perceive polynomial time complexity. Quantum computing, still in its nascent stages, has already showcased its potential through algorithms like Shor's, which promises polynomial-time solutions to problems that were traditionally nestled in the NP-hard category. If quantum computing delivers on its promises, fields like cryptography might undergo seismic shifts. Another direction of interest is parallel computing. With technology ushering in an era dominated by multi-core processors, the potential to further refine and optimize polynomial time algorithms using parallel computing methodologies stands out as a tantalizing prospect.

In summation, by dissecting the various domains where polynomial time complexity plays a pivotal role, we glean a deeper understanding of its indomitable presence in contemporary technology. Whether one is a researcher probing the theoretical depths or a practitioner crafting the next big application, understanding polynomial time complexity is non-negotiable. It's a beacon, guiding algorithmic choices and system designs, ensuring they are not only efficient but also scalable in the face of ever-evolving technological demands.

Value Assessment Computational Framework (VACF)

Chapter 10

Enabling AI Systems to Determine and Compare Values

How do AI systems assess and compare values?

Delving into the intricacies of artificial intelligence and its applications, this chapter unveils a paradigm shift by introducing the Value Assessment Computational Framework (VACF). An innovative leap from the previously discussed Multi-Sensory Computational Framework, the VACF paves the way for AI algorithms to discern, juxtapose, and assign precedence to values using computational techniques. The scope of understanding and applying value assessment spirals into multifaceted realms, encompassing everything from intricate economic matrices to algorithms ingrained with ethical decision-making capabilities.

At the core of the VACF is a foundational belief: values can be quantified and compared in a structured manner. The triad underpinning this framework comprises:

1. Value Units (VU): These are tangible measures encapsulating the essence of an entity's value, meticulously extracted from an array of defining features.
2. Value Factors (VF): Integral parameters these are the touchstones against which an entity's value is gauged. This could span aspects like intrinsic quality, the rarity of occurrence (scarcity), or its utility quotient.

3. Value Relations (VR): Beyond mere value assessment, these sophisticated algorithms are tailored to juxtapose and prioritize values when faced with myriad contexts.

Taking a mathematical dive into the framework, the value, represented as V, of any entity (e) characterized by its features (F) can be comprehensively represented through the equation:
$$V(F) = w1 \cdot f1(F) + w2 \cdot f2(F) + ... + wn \cdot fn(F)$$
Here, wi encapsulates the weightage assigned to discrete value factors represented by fi.

Pivoting to the world of economic systems, the stock market is an illustrative example. Through the lens of the VACF, AI systems are empowered to distill the value of diverse stocks, zeroing in on pivotal factors like the trajectory of growth, associated risks, and overarching market trends. The endgame? Guiding investors by spotlighting investment avenues that promise the most substantial value.

Ethical decision-making algorithms, a domain fraught with complexities, also stand to benefit immensely from the VACF. Consider the case of autonomous vehicles. Often, these machines find themselves at a crossroads where split-second decisions can mean the difference between life and death. By leveraging the VACF, such vehicles can discern the value of varied outcomes, considering multiple facets ranging from the sanctity of human life's potential legal implications to prevalent societal norms and expectations.

Shifting focus to resource allocation, smart grids come to the fore. These grids, designed to be the nerve centers of energy distribution, can harness the VACF to make informed decisions. By evaluating the myriad value factors like the immediacy of demand, operational efficiency, and the consequent environmental footprint, these grids can optimize energy distribution, ensuring resources are channeled where they are most valued.

Healthcare, a domain where decisions can have lasting repercussions, also finds resonance with the VACF. Delving into creating treatment blueprints tailored for individuals, the VACF emerges as a valuable ally. By judiciously evaluating a gamut of medical interventions against criteria like efficacy, financial implications, and patient inclinations, the VACF facilitates the crafting of treatment plans that strike the right balance between medical viability and patient comfort.

The realm of Value Relations is expansive, accommodating a suite of algorithms designed for precise comparisons. For instance:

1. Pairwise Comparison: This straightforward approach juxtaposes the values of two distinct entities, spotlighting the one with superior value. The algorithm can be encapsulated as: $Compare(V(A), V(B)) = \{A$ if $V(A) > V(B)$, B otherwise$\}$.
2. Value Sorting Algorithm: Scaling beyond binary comparisons, this algorithm is designed to categorize a list of entities based on their deduced values. Intricacies of computational efficiency come into play, with typical scenarios operating within the $O(n \log n)$ time complexity bracket.
3. Multi-Objective Optimization: Catering to multifaceted scenarios, this approach grapples with instances where a simultaneous optimization of multiple values is the order of the day.

In summation, the Value Assessment Computational Framework is more than just a theoretical construct; it's a paradigm-shifting methodology that equips AI systems with the tools to quantify and compare values in an informed manner. By grounding the concept of value in quantifiable metrics and pairing it with algorithms tailored for assessment, the VACF promises to redefine decision-making paradigms across a spectrum of domains. Whether it's guiding global investors in the economic arena, assisting physicians in crafting patient-centric treatment plans, or ensuring autonomous vehicles navigate ethical dilemmas with aplomb, the VACF emerges as an indispensable tool in the AI arsenal.

Chapter 11

Integrating Rapid Value Assessment in Computational Systems

How can AI quickly evaluate values?

One of the marvels of the human brain is its astonishing speed at assigning value to objects we perceive. This rapid cognition isn't just a novelty of the human experience; it's deeply rooted in our evolutionary survival instincts. Mirroring this human trait in the realm of artificial intelligence, we introduce the Value Assessment Computational Framework (VACF). This system is informed by a pivotal study by Johns Hopkins University that unveiled a profound discovery: the brain's mechanism for valuing objects is triggered within a mere 80 milliseconds after perceiving them.

Delving deeper into the workings of our cognitive apparatus, this rapid value assessment isn't a standalone process. It takes place almost in tandem with the act of object recognition itself. The journey begins in the visual cortex. Evolutionarily, such rapid cognition was imperative for survival, helping our ancestors make swift decisions in life-threatening scenarios. In designing the VACF, the aspiration is to mirror this remarkable human faculty. At its core, the VACF operates with a conviction: values can be quantified and juxtaposed. It's a multi-faceted structure, encompassing:

1. Visual Recognition Unit (VRU): Emulating the human visual cortex, this unit's mandate is to identify incoming data or objects.

2. Rapid Value Processing Unit (RVPU): This unit, true to its name, swiftly assigns a value tag to an object, resonating with the brain's instantaneous value processing function.

3. Value Units (VU): This serves as the yardstick for quantifying an entity's value, drawing from diverse features.

4. Value Factors (VF): These critical metrics—like quality, rarity, and utility—shape an entity's value.

5. Decision-making Unit (DMU): Once values are assigned and assessed, this unit takes the reins, sculpting suitable responses.

Mathematically, the VACF is a marriage of two models. The first model interweaves the influences of visual recognition and rapid value processing:

$$V(x) = \alpha \times VRU(x) + \beta \times RVPU(x).$$

The second model paints a picture of how different value factors come into play:

$$V(F) = w1 \cdot f1(F) + w2 \cdot f2(F) + \ldots + wn \cdot fn(F).$$

Peering through the prism of practical applications, the VACF's potential is immense. In the world of autonomous vehicles, this framework can be a game-changer, enabling the vehicle's AI to rapidly discern between a pedestrian and an inanimate object like a traffic cone. In the high-octane universe of financial trading, where milliseconds can translate to millions, VACF's capacity for real-time decision-making based on fluctuating financial instrument values can be revolutionary. The medical realm isn't untouched either. Here, the VACF can be pivotal in swiftly differentiating benign cells from malignant ones, leading to timely treatment interventions.

The process of value assessment in VACF also incorporates algorithms such as:

1. Pairwise Comparison: Compare(V(A),V(B)) = {A if V(A) > V(B), B otherwise}.

2. Value Sorting Algorithm: It systematizes entities as per their deduced values, typically in an $O(n\log n)$ timeframe.
3. Multi-Objective Optimization: Tailored for instances where various values need simultaneous optimization.

VACF's significance transcends its components. What we have on our hands is a computational tool that's not just swift, akin to human cognition, but also thorough in analyzing value factors and their interplays. This duality ensures its relevance across myriad domains.

As technology evolves, so does the VACF. Enter VACF 2.0.

The advanced Visual Recognition Unit (VRU 2.0) incorporates state-of-the-art facial recognition technologies like OpenCV. Moreover, it marries this with object recognition algorithms such as YOLO. The unit's mathematical function stands as:
$VRU(x) = \omega1 \times OpenCV(x) + \omega2 \times YOLO(x) + \omega3 \times Luminosity(x)$.

The revamped Rapid Value Processing Unit (RVPU 2.0) harnesses the prowess of neural networks, possibly GPT variants for textual objects, or CNNs for images. It's structured as:
$RVPU(x) = \gamma1 \times NN\text{-}Classifier(x) + \gamma2 \times RL(x) + \gamma3 \times Special\text{-}Heuristic(x)$.

The new Decision-making Unit (DMU 2.0) utilizes decision trees for categorization, and for scenarios with high stakes, like autonomous driving, it aligns with the latest Advanced Driver Assistance Systems (ADAS). Its mathematical representation is:
$DMU(V) = \delta1 \times DecisionTree(V) + \delta2 \times ADAS(V)$.

Pooling these advancements, the VACF 2.0 function is captured as:
$V(x) = \alpha \times VRU(x) + \beta \times RVPU(x) + \gamma \times DMU(V(x))$.

By synergizing contemporary software and hardware advancements, VACF 2.0 not only seeks to mimic human rapid value assessment capabilities but also aims to provide a resilient framework adaptable across sectors.

Chapter 12

Synthesizing the VACF 2.0, MSCF, and RDI Systems

How do these systems come together for a unified brain theory?

Synthesizing the VACF 2.0, MSCF, and RDI Systems into an Advanced AI Behavioral Blueprint paves the way for a new paradigm in artificial intelligence. Merging distinct computational paradigms such as the Value Assessment Computational Framework 2.0 (VACF 2.0), the Multi-Sensory Computational Framework (MSCF), and the Repetition, Duration, and Intensity (RDI) System heralds an age where AI systems exhibit enriched behavioral and decision-making capabilities. Delving into this realm, we unearth the harmonization of these systems to sculpt a refined behavioral model for AI.

Piecing these frameworks together mandates a deep dive into the essence of each module. The VACF 2.0 arms AI with the capability to evaluate and designate value to diverse entities swiftly. Concurrently, MSCF imparts to AI the proficiency to assimilate data across a spectrum of sensory avenues. Contrasting these, the RDI System mirrors the human learning mechanism, enabling AI's grasp of concepts through repetition and modulating its actions based on the persistence and magnitude of stimuli.

Embarking on the mathematical aspect, the amalgamation of these entities is eloquently represented as: $U(x) = \alpha \times VACF2(x) + \beta \times MSCF(x) + \gamma \times RDI(x)$. In this equation, α, β, and γ emerge as balancing coefficients, delicately modulating the influence of each framework. This triad finds its epitome in the decision-making architecture, wherein the MSCF stands at the forefront, amassing sensory data. This data torrent is then funneled into the VACF 2.0, facilitating brisk value extraction. Augmenting this knowledge, the RDI System refines the learning curve and etches the subsequent decision pathways, encapsulated in the modified formula: $DMU(U) = \delta1 \times DecisionTree(U) + \delta2 \times RDI\text{-}Modifier(U)$.

The applicative potential of this integrative framework spans diverse sectors. Within the realms of real-time robotics, machines metamorphose into sentient beings, astutely decoding their environments, orchestrating task hierarchies, and evolving through experiential learning. Transitioning to the healthcare domain, the system exhibits the prowess to incisively dissect voluminous health data, calibrating value metrics to therapeutic interventions, and continually refining its analytical edge with incoming data streams. The financial cosmos isn't untouched either. Beyond the immediate value determinations in fluctuating trading arenas, the architecture exhibits an innate adaptability, resonating with the ever-shifting financial trends.

Diving into the algorithmic corridors, the framework, aided by sorting and graph theory paradigms, gracefully maneuvers multifaceted decision-making scenarios. The Enhanced Pairwise Appraisal algorithm resonates as: $Compare(U(A),U(B)) = \{A$ if $U(A) > U(B)$, else $B\}$. Furthermore, the RDI-infused Multi-objective Optimization reengineers traditional optimization techniques, weaving in the RDI nuances, ensuring adaptability is at the core.

The amalgam's computational prowess is unmistakable. Tailored to cater to the urgency of real-time applications, the synthesized system seamlessly integrates parallel computational strategies and distributed architectures, ensuring brisk and robust operations. Conclusively, this intricate behavioral matrix for AI, birthed from the union of VACF 2.0, MSCF, and the RDI System, redefines adaptability and decision-making benchmarks in AI. It is a beacon of integrative computational thought, promising unparalleled navigation through diverse challenges.

Grand Unified Brain Theory

Chapter 13

Symbolic Representation of Neurobiological Processes in Cognitive Functions

How can we symbolically represent brain processes?

Symbolic Representation of Neurobiological Processes in Cognitive Functions
Mathematical and computational models have increasingly aided the field of neuroscience to describe the complex processes occurring in the brain. These models range from simplified abstractions to detailed biophysical descriptions of neural activity. Utilizing symbolic representation to describe various brain actions provides a powerful framework for understanding and predicting brain functions (Dayan Abbott, 2001; Gerstner, Kistler, Naud, Paninski, 2014).

Voltage Spike Generation by Neurons

The production of voltage spikes by neurons can be mathematically captured using the piecewise function:

$V_n(t) = \{V_{spike}$ *ifaspikeoccursattimet0otherwise*

where $V_n(t)$ denotes the voltage produced by neuron n at time t, and V_{spike} is the voltage level during a spike. This representation is a simplification of the more complex Hodgkin-Huxley model, but provides a foundational understanding of spike generation (Hodgkin Huxley, 1952).

Axonal Pulse Propagation

The propagation of a neural pulse along an axon can be expressed as: $P(t) = V_n(t - \tau)$

where $P(t)$ denotes the pulse at time t, and τ represents the time delay associated with pulse propagation. This model could be extended to include the effects of myelination and axonal diameter on signal speed (Seidl, 2014).

Synaptic Chemical Signal Release

The release of neurotransmitters at the synapse can be described as: $S(t) = \alpha \cdot V_n(t)$

where $S(t)$ is the chemical signal strength at time t, and α is a coefficient translating the voltage to chemical signal strength. This offers a linear approximation to the complex mechanisms of synaptic neurotransmission (Koch, 1999).

Facial Recognition

The cognitive task of recognizing a face can be symbolically represented as: $R(x) = \{1 \ if face is recognized 0 otherwise$

where $R(x)$ is a function of the input x, which could be a multidimensional vector representing the visual data of a face. Recent advances in neural decoding techniques have focused on reconstructing perceived images from brain activity, offering a bridge between this symbolic representation and empirical data (Naselaris et al., 2015).

Memory States

Different types of memory, including short-term, long-term, and declarative memories, can be conceptually represented as a state vector in a memory space:

$$M = Mshort Mlong Mdeclarative$$

Each component of this vector may be subject to different rules for updating and decay, governed by various biochemical and electrical processes (Fuster, 1995; Squire, 2009). In summary, symbolic representations offer a useful lens for conceptualizing complex neurobiological processes. These representations may serve as the foundation for more detailed models, incorporating empirical findings from both experimental and computational neuroscience.

Chapter 14

Extended Symbolic Representations for Cognitive and Neurological Phenomena

How can we expand symbolic representations in cognition?

The complexity of the brain's operations can be further understood through additional symbolic representations that account for various forms of learning, memory dynamics, sensory associations, and baseline activities. These models can build upon foundational concepts in computational neuroscience and cognitive psychology (O'Reilly Munakata, 2000; Friston, 2010).

Learning and Memory as Functions of Brain Structures

Different memory types can be described as functions dependent on various brain structures: $M_i = f_i(B)$

Here, M_i signifies the i-th type of memory, and B represents a vector comprising the relevant brain structures. This perspective aligns with the growing research on the localization and distribution of different memory systems within the brain (Eichenbaum, 2017).

Synaptic Changes for Memory Storage

The strengthening or weakening of synaptic connections, fundamental to memory storage, can be modeled as:

$$S_{ij}(t) = w \cdot A_i(t) \cdot A_j(t)$$

In this equation, $S_{ij}(t)$ denotes the strength of the synaptic connection between neurons i and j at time t, while $A_i(t)$ and $A_j(t)$ represent their respective neural activities. The term w serves as a weight parameter. This formula encapsulates the essence of Hebbian learning rules, which are pivotal in synaptic plasticity (Hebb, 1949).

Associations and Sensory Triggers
Associative learning can be represented by a vector $\mathbf{C}$ that encapsulates various sensations:

An associated triggering equation is:

$$\mathbf{C} = CsmellCtasteCcolorCfeel \ \mathbf{C}_{trigger} = \mathbf{M} \cdot \mathbf{C}$$

Here, $\mathbf{M}$ is a matrix that signifies how one sensation can evoke another. This formulation offers a mathematical perspective on classical conditioning paradigms (Pavlov, 1927).

Encoding Relationships

Encoding can be abstractly represented by a function that captures relationships between elements: $E(\mathbf{r}) = \mathbf{R}$

In this expression, $\mathbf{r}$ is a vector containing raw data, while $\mathbf{R}$ is a vector of relationships between these elements. This concept aligns with theories of relational memory (Cohen Eichenbaum, 1993).

Memory Retrieval

The process of memory retrieval can be modeled as:
$$\mathbf{m} = R(\mathbf{q})$$

Here, $\mathbf{m}$ is the retrieved memory and $\mathbf{q}$ is the query. This symbolic representation could include probabilistic or dynamic retrieval

aspects   (Anderson,   1983).
Memory Destabilization

The transient destabilization of memory can be expressed as: M_{temp} = $D(\mathbf{m})$

Here, M_{temp} represents the temporarily destabilized memory, and D is a function denoting the destabilization process. This equation resonates with research on memory reconsolidation (Nader, Schafe, Le Doux, 2000).

Baseline Brain Activity

Baseline neural activity can be described by the function: $B(t) = k \cdot R(t) + b$

In this equation, $B(t)$ denotes the baseline brain activity at time t, $R(t)$ indicates restructuring or simulating knowledge, k is a scaling constant, and b represents other baseline activities. This formulation can incorporate fluctuating baseline activities observed in resting-state networks (Raichle, 2015).

Chapter 15

Further Expansions in Symbolic Representations of Neurocognitive Processes

What more can be represented in neurocognition?

To comprehensively model the rich tapestry of cognitive and neurobiological processes, we extend the symbolic framework to include task-oriented behavior, perception, dreaming, and predictive faculties. These mathematical models aim to capture the multi-faceted nature of mental activities and are influenced by contemporary research in neuroscience and cognitive science (Friston, 2009; Hassabis Maguire, 2009).

Preparatory Activity Reduction for Goal-Directed Tasks

The rate of change in baseline neural activity before executing a goal directed task can be represented as: $B'(t) = -\delta \cdot G(t)$

Here, $B'(t)$ is the rate of change of baseline activity, $G(t)$ is a function describing the goal-directed task, and δ is a constant determining the rate of activity decrease. This model can be interpreted in light of research on preparatory activity in neural networks (Bastian et al., 2003).

Sensory Input and Internal Experience Perceived sensory

experience can be described by: $P(t) = S(t) + I(t)$

In this equation, $P(t)$ is the perceived experience at time t, $S(t)$ is the internal sensory state, and $I(t)$ is the external sensory input. This reflects theories suggesting that perception is a function of both external stimuli and internal states (Chalmers, 1996). Awake and Dream States

The *awake state* can be modeled as a weighted combination of the dreaming state and external stimuli: $A(t) = D(t) + \varepsilon \cdot E(t)$

Here, $A(t)$ is the awake state at time t, $D(t)$ represents the dreaming state, $E(t)$ is external stimuli, and ε is a constant. This model aligns with theories of dreaming as a form of proto consciousness (Hobson, 2009).

Emulating Possible Futures

The emulation of possible future states can be represented as: $F(t,a) = E(S(t),a)$

In this representation, $F(t,a)$ is the future state at time t given an action a, $S(t)$ is the current state, and E is an emulation function. This is relevant to discussions on mental time travel and planning (Schacter, Addis, Buckner, 2007).

Internal Representations of External Reality

The brain's internal model of the external world can be encapsulated by:
$M(t) = I(t) \cdot R$

Here, $M(t)$ is the internal model at time t, $I(t)$ is the sensory input, and R is a matrix that formalizes the relationships between various elements in the external world. This is consistent with theories of internal models in cognition (Wolpert, Ghahramani, Jordan, 1995).

Perception as Expectation Matching

Perception can be modeled as a matching process between incoming sensory data and internal expectations:

$$P(t) = M(I(t), E(t))$$

Here, $P(t)$ is the perceived experience at time t, $I(t)$ is incoming sensory data, $E(t)$ is internally generated expectations, and M is a matching function.
This notion is foundational to predictive coding theories of brain function (Rao Ballard, 1999).

Memory for Predictive Functions

Memory can be conceptualized as a tool for generating predictions, expressed as: $\Pi(t) = P(M(t))$

In this equation, $\Pi(t)$ is the prediction at time t, $M(t)$ is the memory at that time, and P is a function converting memories into predictions. This representation extends theories that posit memory as an essential element in future planning and prediction (Bar, 2009).

Chapter 16

Emotional Dimensions in Symbolic Representations of Neurocognitive Phenomena

How are emotions symbolically represented in AI?

Integrating emotional components into mathematical models of brain functions contributes to a more comprehensive understanding of cognitive and affective processes. In this context, we introduce new symbolic representations that capture the role of emotions and feelings in cognition, rooted in contemporary neuroscience and psychology perspectives (Damasio, 1994; LeDoux, 1996).

Special Subtype of Emulation: Memory of Life Events

A specialized form of the emulation function, tailored to represent memories of life events, can be expressed as:

$$F_{life}(t,a) = E(S(t),a;constraints)$$

Here, constraints are introduced to ensure that the emulation progresses in a manner consistent with life experiences. This resonates with theories positing that episodic memories may serve as a basis for simulating future events (Schacter et al., 2008).

Emotions as Physical Responses to Stimuli

Emotions can be modeled as a response function to various stimuli, and are represented as: $E(t) = R(S(t))$

In this equation, $E(t)$ is the emotion at time t, $S(t)$ represents the stimulus, and R is a function mapping stimuli to physical reactions such as heart rate or perspiration. This formulation is aligned with the James- Lange theory of emotion (James, 1884; Lange, 1885).

Feelings as Subjective Transformations of Emotions

The subjective nature of feelings can be captured by transforming physical emotions into subjective experiences:

$$F(t) = F(E(t))$$

Here, $F(t)$ signifies the feeling at time t, and F is a function translating physical emotions into subjective experiences. This concept is informed by theories distinguishing between emotions and feelings (Damasio, 1999).

Emotions as Computational Drivers of Action

The role of emotions in guiding actions can be formalized as: $A(t) = C(E(t), O(t))$

In this equation, $A(t)$ is the action at time t, $O(t)$ represents the outcome, and C is a function that incorporates emotions and anticipated outcomes to determine actions. This is consistent with models positing that emotions serve as computations for action selection (Cosmides Tooby, 2000).

Emotional Influence on Perception

The influence of emotion on perception can be represented as: $P'(t) = P(t) + \alpha \cdot E(t)$

Here, $P'(t)$ is the modified perception at time t, and α is a constant denoting the strength of emotional influence. This formulation acknowledges that emotional states can modulate perception (Phelps et al., 2006).

Emotional Memory Systems

The role of emotions in memory encoding and retrieval can be described as: $M_{emo}(t) = M(E(t), M(t))$

In this equation, $M_{emo}(t)$ represents emotional memory at time t, and M is a function combining emotional and other types of memory. This aligns with studies on the emotional modulation of memory (McGaugh, 2004).

Emotional Disorders as Perturbations in Emotional Systems

Emotional disorders can be modeled as disruptions in the emotional system: $D(t) = D(E(t))$

Here, $D(t)$ symbolizes the disorder at time t, and D is a function mapping from emotions to emotional disorders. This conceptualization is consistent with research on affective disorders (Kendler et al., 2003).

Chapter 17

Representations of Neurocognitive Functions

How is intelligence integrated into symbolic AI representations?

Incorporating dimensions of intelligence significantly amplifies the complexity of our mathematical models of the brain. These extended representations facilitate the exploration of how intelligence manifests through neural activities, storage of information, and the simulation of new situations, informed by current understandings in neuroscience and cognitive psychology (Gazzaniga, 2004; Duncan, 2013).

Intelligence as Manipulation of Knowledge

The manipulation of knowledge by neurons can be described as: $K'(t) = I_K(K(t), N(t), S(t))$

In this model, $K'(t)$ represents the new state of knowledge at time t, $K(t)$ is the existing state of knowledge, $N(t)$ is the neuronal state, and $S(t)$ is the simulation state. The function I_K symbolizes how neurons manipulate knowledge to arrive at new understandings. This is consistent with theories that equate intelligence with the ability to adapt and manipulate information (Sternberg, 1985).

Intelligence as Novel Situation Simulation

The capacity to simulate novel situations is captured by:
$$S'(t) = I_S(S(t), N(t))$$

Here, $S'(t)$ represents the new simulation state at time t, and I_S is a function depicting how neurons simulate new scenarios. This aligns with the construct of fluid intelligence, which involves the ability to solve new problems independent of acquired knowledge (Cattell, 1971).

Intelligence as Storage of Information

The storage, distillation, and retrieval of information by intelligence can be described as: $I'(t) = I_I(I(t), D(t))$

In this equation, $I'(t)$ is the new state of stored information at time t, and I_I represents the relevant intelligent processes. This captures the aspect of crystallized intelligence, which involves the accumulation and retrieval of learned knowledge (Horn Cattell, 1966).

Intelligence and Artificial Intelligence

The progress in artificial intelligence (AI) can be modeled as a function over time: $AI(t) = \beta \cdot Iprinciples + \gamma \cdot Ineurons$

Here, β and γ are constants, while $I_{principles}$ and $I_{neurons}$ represent our understanding of brain principles and the simulation capabilities of neurons, respectively. This encapsulates the dual nature of progress in AI: conceptual advances and computational fidelity (Russell Norvig, 2016).

Complexity of Intelligence as an Integral Function

The multifaceted nature of intelligence suggests that a single mechanism does not underpin it. Therefore, we introduce a composite function to represent the complexity:

$Intelligence(t) = I_m(t)dm$

Z

mechanisms

In this formulation, $I_m(t)$ represents different potential intelligence mechanisms. This model allows for the integration of various aspects, consistent with the notion that intelligence is a complex construct comprising multiple abilities (Gardner, 1983).

Chapter 18

Extending Symbolic Models of Neurocognitive Processes

How do time, sleep, and coding fit into symbolic AI models?

The endeavor to model neurocognitive processes such as intelligence and emotion can be further extended to incorporate various other facets like time perception, sleep, specialized brain systems, consciousness, and neural coding of information. These extensions are informed by empirical evidence and current theories in neuroscience and psychology (Eagleman, 2008; Siegel, 2005; Koch, 2004).

Comparison to Other Species

Intelligence in different species may necessitate distinct mathematical models, accommodating unique aspects such as abstraction and open-ended problem solving in humans. This is consistent with comparative cognition research emphasizing different cognitive architectures across species (Shettleworth, 2010).

Time Representation in the Brain

The perceptual integration of auditory and visual signals for time representation can be modeled as: $T(t) = \alpha \cdot A(t) + \beta \cdot V(t)$

Here, α and β are constants calibrated to account for the typical 30-millisecond difference between auditory and visual processing speeds. This model aligns with studies on multi-sensory integration and time perception (Fujisaki Nishida, 2009).

Sleep and Dreaming

A composite function encapsulating various theories on the function of sleep is: $S(t) = \omega \cdot R(t) + \varphi \cdot L(t) + \theta \cdot M(t)$

This model integrates the restorative nature of sleep, memory consolidation, and the possibility of mental simulations (Tononi Cirelli, 2006).

Specialized Systems in the Brain

Given the brain's specialized systems, their combined activity can be represented as:

$$\sum_{i=1}^{N} C(t) = {}^{x}w_i \cdot A_i(t)$$

This is consistent with distributed coding theories that posit that cognition emerges from coordinated activity across specialized networks (Mesulam, 1998). Consciousness Consciousness can be represented as a function of active and passive neuronal processes:

$$Con(t) = \lambda \cdot Nactive(t) - \mu \cdot Npassive(t) \text{ 18}$$

This model lends itself to theories that differentiate between active and passive states in contributing to consciousness (Dehaene Changeux, 2011).

Sleep-Wake Cycle

The sleep-wake cycle can be represented by a sigmoid function:

This model reflects the biological circadian rhythms governing sleep and wakefulness (Borb'ely Achermann, 1999).

REM Sleep and Memory Consolidation

The state of memory consolidation dependent on REM sleep is modeled as:

This is congruent with theories suggesting a role of REM sleep in memory consolidation (Stickgold, 2005).

Coding Information in Spiking Rates

The rate of spiking in neurons can be modeled as a function of external features: $R(t) = f(F)$

This is consistent with rate coding theories in neuroscience (Gerstner et al., 2014). Neural Networks for Complex Phenomena

Complex phenomena like value judgments can be modeled as:

$$M$$
$$Si = \varphi(Xwij \cdot Nj)\, j=1$$

This captures the essence of artificial neural networks applied to model complex cognitive phenomena.

Chapter 19

Models for Memory Storage, Emotional Processing, and Baseline Brain Activity

How can math model memory, emotion, and brain activity?

The endeavor to develop comprehensive mathematical models of brain function must consider several aspects, including memory storage, emotional processing, and the brain's baseline activity. These models are inspired by empirical evidence and theoretical frameworks in neuroscience and psychology (Hebb, 1949; LeDoux, 2000; McClelland et al., 1995).

Neural Population Coding

In population coding, a pattern P is represented across n neurons as $P = (R_1, R_2, ..., R_n)$, where each neuron contributes its spike rate R_i to form the overall pattern. This model is supported by research in neural coding techniques (Georgopoulos et al., 1986).

Cortical Connectivity

Given the extensive connectivity in the cortex, the effective input I to a neuron can be modeled as , where w_j are synaptic weights and S_j are signal strengths from connecting neurons.

This is consistent with studies on the large-scale connectivity of cortical neurons (Sporns, 2011).

Alternative Signaling Mechanisms

To account for the role of glial cells and biochemical cascades, the total information $T(t)$ can be modeled as $T(t) = \alpha \cdot R(t) + \beta \cdot G(t) + \gamma \cdot B(t)$. These terms are weighted by constants α, β, γ, indicative of the importance of each signaling mechanism (Araque et al., 1999; Purves et al., 2018).

Memory Storage: Synaptic Trace Model

The Synaptic Trace Model posits that memories are formed through synaptic strengthening between co- active neurons. The change in synaptic weight Δw_{ij} can be expressed as $\Delta w_{ij} = \eta \cdot (A_i \cdot A_j)$, embodying Hebbian learning principles ("Cells that fire together, wire together") (Hebb, 1949).

Types and Structures of Memory

Memory types and their associated neural structures can be represented   as), where $f(\tau, T)$ denotes how the type and structure of the memory affect its formation (Eichenbaum, 2000).

Memory Associations and Relational Encoding

The relational aspect of memory can be captured by $M_{rel} = P_{i,j}$ $w_{ij} \cdot R(i,j)$, highlighting the role of synaptic weights in encoding relationships between items (Cohen Eichenbaum, 1993).

$$I = \sum_{j=1}^{10,000} w_j \cdot S_j$$
$$M(t, \tau, T) = \sum_{i=1}^{n} \Delta w_{ij} \cdot f(\tau, T$$

Memory Retrieval and Destabilization

Memory retrieval can be modeled as $Answer = \rho(Q,M)$, where ρ is a retrieval function scanning memory M based on a query Q. During retrieval, memories may be destabilized, represented by $\Delta M = -\delta \cdot \rho(Q,M)$ (Nader et al., 2000).

Baseline Brain Activity

The brain's baseline activity $B(t)$ can be modeled as $B(t) = \alpha \cdot R(t) + \beta \cdot E(t) + \gamma \cdot F(t)$, incorporating ongoing cognitive functions like restructuring of knowledge $R(t)$, emotional processing $E(t)$, and future simulations $F(t)$ (Raichle et al., 2001).

Task-Specific Deactivation and Resource Allocation

Prior to task engagement, certain brain regions show reduced activity, modeled by $D(t,G) = B(t) - \varphi \cdot G(t)$. This model underscores the concept of resource allocation (Fox et al., 2005).

Sensory Input as Modifier

Sensory input $S(t)$ may serve as a modifier to baseline activity, represented by $B'(t) = B(t) + \lambda \cdot S(t)$ (Lamme Roelfsema, 2000).

Dreaming and Awake States

Dreaming and awake states can be represented along a continuum as $D(t) = \theta \cdot B(t) + (1-\theta) \cdot S(t)$, balancing the influence of sensory input $S(t)$ on baseline activity $B(t)$ (Hobson, 2009).

Brain as Prognosticator

The brain's ability to simulate futures is captured by $F(t) = \delta \cdot S(t) + (1 - \delta) \cdot M(t)$, emphasizing the role of memories in predictive algorithms (Schacter et al., 2007).

Emotional Processing

Emotional states $E(t)$ can be modeled as $E(t) = \sigma \cdot V(o) + (1-\sigma) \cdot R(s)$, incorporating the value of outcomes $V(o)$ and physiological responses $R(s)$ (Damasio, 1994).

Emotional Disorders

The mathematical representation of emotional disorders, potentially involving neurochemical imbalances or flawed connectivity, remains an active area of research, with implications for understanding conditions like depression and anxiety (Davidson et al., 2002).

These mathematical models serve as foundational structures for understanding complex neurocognitive processes, offering a systematic approach for the scientific community. The aspiration for a" Grand Unified Theory" of brain function remains an ambitious but worthwhile scientific pursuit.

Chapter 20

A High-Level Equation for Integrating Multifaceted Brain Functions

Can we create a single equation for all brain functions?

The ambition to encapsulate the complexities of brain function into a unified mathematical framework necessitates incorporating many variables. My proposed equation,

$$\textit{BrainFunction} = \alpha \cdot NCA + \beta \cdot MSR + \gamma \cdot BA + \delta \cdot FS + \varepsilon \cdot EMO + \zeta \cdot INT + \eta \cdot T + \theta \cdot SD + \iota \cdot SSI + \kappa \cdot CON,$$

adeptly incorporates various elements that contribute to overall brain function. Here, each term represents a specific aspect, and the coefficients $\alpha, \beta, \gamma, \delta, \varepsilon, \zeta, \eta, \theta, \iota, \kappa$ serve as weighting factors. As you suggested, these coefficients could be dynamic, adapting to contextual changes, internal states, or external stimuli.

Neural Coding Activity (*NCA*)
The term *NCA* could encapsulate various aspects of neural coding, such as rate, temporal, and population (Pouget et al., 2000).

$$NCA = f(R(t), T(t), P)$$

Memory Storage and Retrieval (*MSR*)
MSR would integrate memory storage processes, relational encoding, and retrieval mechanisms (Tulving Craik, 2000).

$$MSR = g(\Delta w_{ij}, M_{rel}, \rho(Q, M))$$

Baseline Activity (*BA*)
The term *BA* may incorporate the brain's idling activity, which is far from inactive and includes various ongoing cognitive functions (Raichle et al., 2001).

$$BA = h(R(t), E(t), F(t))$$

Future Simulation (*FS*)
FS would encapsulate the brain's ability to simulate future scenarios, based on sensory input and stored memories (Schacter et al., 2007).

$$FS = i(S(t), M(t))$$

Emotional State (*EMO*)
EMO could be a composite function of multiple variables reflecting an individual's emotional state, such as physiological responses and emotional memories (LeDoux, 2000).

$$EMO = j(V(o), R(s), M_{emo})$$

Intelligence (*INT*)
This term would incorporate various dimensions of intelligence, including knowledge manipulation, novel situation simulation, and information storage (Sternberg, 1999).

$INT = k(K'(t),S'(t),I'(t))$
T would encapsulate how the brain synchronizes auditory and visual signals to create a perception of time

Time Representation (T) (Merchant et al., 2013).

$T = l(A(t),V(t))$
SD would capture various theories and dimensions of sleep, including restorative aspects and memory

Sleep and Dreams (SD) consolidation (Walker, 2009).

$SD = m(R(t),L(t),M(t))$
SSI could represent the coordination of activity levels across various specialized systems within the brain

Specialized Systems Integration (SSI) (Sporns, 2011).

$SSI = n(A_i(t))$
Finally, CON would incorporate active and passive neuronal processes that contribute to conscious

Consciousness (CON)
experience (Dehaene et al., 2017).

$$CON = o(Nactive,Npassive)$$

This integrative equation aims to offer a comprehensive yet tractable framework for understanding brain function. It holds the promise of harmonizing disparate areas of neuroscience, psychology, and even artificial intelligence, into a coherent theoretical structure. Future empirical studies would be essential to calibrate the weights and validate the functional forms of these terms.

Chapter 21

Summary Exploring the Composite Functions of Brain Activity

What have we learned about the brain's composite functions?

Neural Coding Activity (*NCA*) The function *NCA(V,N,C,G)* encapsulates the complex interplay between voltage spikes *V* , the number of neurons *N*, cortical connections *C*, and the role of glial cells *G*. These factors collectively contribute to the rate and pattern of neural firing, which encodes information (Liu and Wang, 2001).

Memory Storage and Retrieval (*MSR*) The function *MSR(T,S,E,Q)* models the role of memory types *T*, synaptic involvement *S*, encoding mechanisms *E*, and retrieval speed *Q*. Each of these factors plays a critical role in the formation, storage, and retrieval of memories (Eichenbaum, 2017).

Baseline Activity (*BA*) The *BA(O,R,E,D)* function incorporates the brain's oxygen consumption *O*, knowledge restructuring *R*, influence of external stimuli *E*, and awake dreaming *D*. These elements collectively contribute to the brain's baseline or 'resting' activity (Raichle, 2015).

Future Simulation (*FS*) The function *FS(P,M,I,A)* incorporates predictive capabilities *P*, internal models *M*, internal expectations *I*, and the Aristotelian concept of memory *A* as a tool for future simulation (Schacter and Addis, 2007).

Emotional State (*EMO*) The *EMO(V,U,C,R)* function encompasses value assignment V , unconscious mechanisms U, cultural influences C, and related disorders R. Each of these variables contributes to the complex landscape of human emotions (LeDoux, 2012).

This framework, although a simplification, offers a structured approach to understanding the multifaceted nature of brain activity. Each function could indeed be a deeply nested equation itself, capturing a myriad of factors and subfactors. Additionally, the equations can be nonlinear, dynamic, and adaptive, subject to temporal and experiential changes.

Applications to Artificial Intelligence
Predictive Modeling Incorporating predictive abilities akin to the brain's future simulation could result in AI systems that are proactive rather than merely reactive. Long Short-Term Memory (LSTM) networks could be further refined to emulate the brain's internal predictive models (Hochreiter and Schmidhuber, 1997).

Neuromorphic Computing Advancements in understanding neural coding could lead to the development of neuromorphic chips that mimic brain-like information processing, potentially surpassing the efficiency of traditional microprocessors for specific tasks (Mead, 1990).
Affective Computing Emulating the emotional landscape of the brain could lead to more empathetic AI systems capable of recognizing and interpreting human emotions (Picard, 1997).

Multi-Modal Learning The brain's adeptness at synchronizing multiple sensory inputs could inform the development of AI systems capable of integrating data from various modalities, enhancing their decision- making capabilities (Baltrusaitis et al., 2019).

Dynamic Memory Allocation Understanding the brain's selective memory encoding could revolutionize AI memory storage, enabling dynamic resource allocation based on task importance (Kanerva, 1988).

Cognitive AI Incorporating facets of human intelligence could lead to AI systems capable of handling complex tasks that require intuition, imagination, or the ability to manage ambiguous data (Marcus, 2018).

Conscious Agents While recreating consciousness in AI remains controversial, insights into its material underpinnings could guide the development of agents with rudimentary self-awareness or introspection (Dehaene et al., 2017).

Real-Time Processing and Integration Emulating the brain's ability to rapidly integrate disparate functions could produce AI systems that excel in real-time data processing, a critical trait for various applications such as autonomous vehicles and financial markets (Mnih et al., 2015).

Sleep and Rejuvenation Algorithms The brain's sleep function, potentially involved in memory consolidation, could inspire algorithms that allow AI systems to optimize their parameters during low- power modes (Hinton et al., 1995).

Context-Aware Processing Mimicking the brain's baseline activity could result in AI systems better equipped for context-aware processing and long-term planning (Bengio et al., 2013).

In summary, the proposed Grand Unified Theory of Brain Function holds significant potential for advancing our understanding of the brain and has myriad applications in the realm of artificial intelligence.

To realize this promise, interdisciplinary efforts involving neuroscience, cognitive psychology, computer science, and data science would be essential.

Conclusion

As we reach the end of this monumental journey through the labyrinth of neural pathways and computational equations, one cannot help but appreciate the vastness of human cognition and its immense potential for technological applications. This book has strived to present a comprehensive toolkit for scholars and practitioners in decoding the brain's complexities through mathematical models. However, it is important to acknowledge that the frontiers of neuroscience and AI are continuously expanding. The models and formulas in this book offer a solid foundation, but they are merely the tip of the iceberg. I encourage scholars to build upon this work, Bine-tuning and augmenting these mathematical representations to adapt to new discoveries and challenges.

References

- O'Reilly, R. C., & Munakata, Y. (2000). Computational explorations in cognitive neuroscience: Understanding the mind by simulating the brain. MIT press.

- Friston, K. (2010). The free-energy principle: a unified brain theory? Nature reviews neuroscience, 11(2), 127-138.

- Eichenbaum, H. (2017). Memory: Organization and control. Annual Review of Psychology, 68, 19-45.

- Hebb, D. O. (1949). The organization of behavior. Wiley.

- Pavlov, I. P. (1927). Conditioned reflexes. Oxford University Press.

- Cohen, N. J., & Eichenbaum, H. (1993). Memory, amnesia, and the hippocampal system. MIT press.

- Anderson, J. R. (1983). Retrieval of information from long-term memory. Science, 220(4592), 25-30.

- Nader, K., Schafe, G. E., & Le Doux, J. E. (2000). Fear memories require protein synthesis in the amygdala for reconsolidation after retrieval. Nature, 406(6797), 722-726.

- Raichle, M. E. (2015). The restless brain: how intrinsic activity organizes brain function. Philosophical Transactions of the Royal Society B: Biological Sciences, 370(1668), 20140172.

- Friston, K. (2009). The free-energy principle: a rough guide to the brain? Trends in cognitive sciences, 13(7), 293-301.

- Hassabis, D., & Maguire, E. A. (2009). The construction system of the brain. Philosophical Transactions of the Royal Society B: Biological Sciences, 364(1521), 1263-1271.

- Bastian, A., Schöner, G., & Riehle, A. (2003). Preshaping and continuous evolution of motor cortical representations during movement preparation. The European Journal of Neuroscience, 18(7), 2047-2058.

- Chalmers, D. J. (1996). The conscious mind: In search of a fundamental theory. Oxford University Press.

- Hobson, J. A. (2009). REM sleep and dreaming: towards a theory of protoconsciousness. Nature Reviews Neuroscience, 10(11), 803-813.

- Schacter, D. L., Addis, D. R., & Buckner, R. L. (2007). Remembering the past to imagine the future: the prospective brain. Nature Reviews Neuroscience, 8(9), 657-661.

- Wolpert, D. M., Ghahramani, Z., & Jordan, M. I. (1995). An internal model for sensorimotor integration. Science, 269(5232), 1880-1882.

- Rao, R. P., & Ballard, D. H. (1999). Predictive coding in the visual cortex: a functional interpretation of some extra-classical receptive-field effects. Nature neuroscience, 2(1), 79-87.

- Bar, M. (2009). The proactive brain: memory for predictions. Philosophical Transactions of the Royal Society B: Biological Sciences, 364(1521), 1235-1243.

- Damasio, A. R. (1994). Descartes' error: Emotion, reason, and the human brain. G.P. Putnam's Sons.

- LeDoux, J. (1996). The emotional brain: The mysterious underpinnings of emotional life. Simon and Schuster.

- Schacter, D. L., Addis, D. R., & Buckner, R. L. (2008). Episodic simulation of future events: concepts, data, and applications. Annals of the New York Academy of Sciences, 1124(1), 39-60.

- James, W. (1884). What is an emotion? Mind, 9(34), 188-205.

- Lange, C. G. (1885). The mechanism of the emotions. The classical psychologists, 672-684.

- Damasio, A. (1999). The feeling of what happens: Body and emotion in the making of consciousness. Harcourt Brace.

- Cosmides, L., & Tooby, J. (2000). Evolutionary psychology and the emotions. Handbook of emotions, 2, 91-115.

- Phelps, E. A., Ling, S., & Carrasco, M. (2006). Emotion facilitates perception and potentiates the perceptual benefits of attention. Psychological science, 17(4), 292-299.

- McGaugh, J. L. (2004). The amygdala modulates the consolidation of memories of emotionally arousing experiences. Annual review of neuroscience, 27, 1-28.

- Kendler, K. S., Gardner, C. O., & Prescott, C. A. (2003). Toward a comprehensive developmental model for major depression in men. American Journal of Psychiatry, 160(1), 143-150.

- Rumelhart, D. E., Hinton, G. E., & Williams, R. J. (1986). Learning representations by back-propagating errors. Nature, 323(6088), 533-536.

- Pouget, A., Dayan, P., & Zemel, R. (2000). Information processing with population codes. Nature Reviews Neuroscience, 1(2), 125-132.

- Tulving, E., & Craik, F. I. M. (Eds.). (2000). The Oxford Handbook of Memory. Oxford University Press.

- Raichle, M. E., MacLeod, A. M., Snyder, A. Z., Powers, W. J., Gusnard, D. A., & Shulman, G. L. (2001). A default mode of brain function. Proceedings of the National Academy of Sciences, 98(2), 676-682.

- Schacter, D. L., Addis, D. R., & Buckner, R. L. (2007). Remembering the past to imagine the future: the prospective brain. Nature Reviews Neuroscience, 8(9), 657-661.

- LeDoux, J. E. (2000). Emotion circuits in the brain. Annual Review of Neuroscience, 23(1), 155-184.

- Sternberg, R. J. (1999). Intelligence as developing expertise. Contemporary Educational Psychology, 24(4), 359-375.

- Merchant, H., Harrington, D. L., & Meck, W. H. (2013). Neural basis of the perception and estimation of time. Annual Review of Neuroscience, 36, 313-336.

Made in the USA
Columbia, SC
02 January 2025

48674605R00048